All This and Snoopy, Too

Charles M. Schulz

Selected cartoons from
YOU CAN'T WIN, CHARLIE BROWN, Vol. I

CORONET BOOKS
Hodder Fawcett, London

Copyright © 1960, 1961, 1962 by United Feature
Syndicate, Inc.
First published by Fawcett Publications Inc.,
New York.
Coronet edition 1969
Eighth impression 1975

This book is sold subject to the condition that
it shall not, by way of trade or otherwise, be
lent, re-sold, hired out or otherwise circulated
without the publisher's prior consent in any
form of binding or cover other than that in
which this is published and without a similar
condition including this condition being
imposed on the subsequent purchaser.

Printed and bound in Great Britain for
Coronet Books,
Hodder Paperbacks Ltd,
St. Paul's House, Warwick Lane,
London, EC4P 4AH
by Hazell Watson & Viney Ltd
Aylesbury, Bucks

ISBN 0 34 04405 5

ALL OF EARTH'S CREATURES
HAVE, HIDDEN WITHIN THEIR
BEINGS, A WILD UNCONTROLLABLE
URGE TO **PUNT**!

PSYCHIATRIC
HELP 5¢
MODERN METHODS

© 1970 United Feature Syndicate, Inc.

Wherever Paperbacks Are Sold

HERE COMES SNOOPY - FROM CORONET

Peanuts
CHARLES M. SCHULZ

All these books are available at your local bookshop or newsagent, or can be ordered direct from the publisher. Just tick the titles you want and fill in the form below.

Prices and availability subject to change without notice.

....

CORONET BOOKS, P.O. Box 11, Falmouth, Cornwall.

Please send cheque or postal order, and allow the following for postage and packing:

U.K.—One book 18p plus 8p per copy for each additional book ordered, up to a maximum of 66p.

B.F.P.O. and EIRE—18p for the first book plus 8p per copy for the next 6 books, thereafter 3p per book.

OTHER OVERSEAS CUSTOMERS—20p for the first book and 10p per copy for each additional book.

Name...

Address..

....